Potted History

It was a bumpy ride on touchdown at Geneva on a hot Summer's day in 1949. And as we careered forwards at 80 mph, the Viking's engines were promptly switched off. Clearly, something had gone badly wrong. If we were going to end up in a heap, then silent engines reduced the risk of fire. The undercarriage was taking a hammering, and we had enough fuel left to cause mayhem if the undercarriage collapsed. This would puncture the nacelle tanks, pouring fuel over two hot engines. But Vickers had designed a robust aircraft, nothing broke and eventually the Viking came to a halt, slewing round as it did so in a manoeuvre that further stressed the undercarriage. A burst starboard tyre had driven the Viking off the runway on to the grass.

If handsome is as handsome does, then the British-built Vickers Viking should have been a failure. But it was no such thing and it sold in numbers similar to the highly-rated American Convair 240. A stopgap airliner in every sense, the twin-engine VC1 Viking was introduced in 1945 to meet post-war British medium-haul needs, until more modern airliners became available. The Viking resulted from a Ministry of Supply and Aircraft Production order, placed in October 1944, for three Wellington Transport Aircraft to meet Specification 17/44.

When the Viking was designed, all-metal stressed skin construction was normal for this class of aircraft, and the Viking was planned to have this construction throughout. But time was saved by initially using fabric-covered, metal-framed geodetic wings similar to those of the existing Wellington bomber, as well as Wellington based engines and landing gear, all fitted to a new 21-seater all-metal fuselage.

Joseph "Mutt" Summers flew the prototype, G-AGOK, for the first time from Wisley, Surrey, on 22 June 1945, shortly after the end of WW2 in Europe. Two more prototypes were built as G-AGOL and G-AGOM. The Viking was the first post-war British medium-haul airliner, although its reliance on Wellington-derived components made it more like fairly new wine in an old bottle. However, this was an advantage, because the Viking had many proven features in its design, including its proven Bristol Hercules radials, over 57,000 of which had been built since 1936,

The Viking's conservative design made it prematurely dated when it entered service, because modern airliners were then being introduced with features such as tricycle undercarriages, reversible pitch propellers and pressurised accommodation, none of which the Viking had. The Viking was, however, designed to meet the new International Civil Aviation Authority (ICAO) standards for single-engine operation. The prototype Viking was powered by two 1,675 hp Bristol Hercules 130 engines, whose single-speed superchargers were adequate for the Viking's moderate operating altitudes of around 8,000 ft (2,440 m).

The prototype Viking's Hercules engines dispensed with the Bristol company's characteristic leading edge exhaust collector ring. Instead, the exhaust system comprised several short pipes behind the engine cowling. But the classic Bristol system was fitted to early production Vikings; later aircraft had exhaust rings mounted behind the engines.

The pro[tot...])6 kg) and cruised [...] of 89 ft 3 in (27.2[...]) were roughly the same as the dimens[...] Douglas DC-3, but the Viking had 40 per cent more power than the Pratt & Whitney-engined DC-3.

The Ministry of Aircraft Production ordered 50 Vikings on 5 April 1946, and the type received its Certificate of Airworthiness on 24 April. It seemed probable that Railway Air Services (RAS) would be the Viking's first operator. The company was formed in 1934 by Imperial Airways and the four major, privately owned railway companies, the Great Western Railway (GWR), London Midland and Scottish Railway (LMS), Southern Railway (SR) and London and North Eastern Railway (LNER)

RAS operated an extensive internal route network in the UK during the 'thirties and, after WW2, the firm planned to extend services to the Continent for which Vikings would be ideal. But Clement Attlee's post-war Labour government formed British European Airways (BEA) in 1946, and this state-owned company took over RAS on 1 February 1947, so the Vikings intended for RAS went to BEA instead.

The 19 Viking 498 Mk 1As, early production versions, had fabric-covered geodetic wings and tail surfaces. Instead of the prototype's Herc 130 engines these aircraft had 1,690 hp Hercules 630 engines, still with single speed superchargers.

Of these Vikings, whose 498 type number reflected the tailoring of aircraft to meet customers' individual needs, the first eight did not serve as airliners with BEA. G-AGON, the first production Viking, joined the third prototype at the BEA Division of BOAC for development flying. The next seven production aircraft also joined the Division as G-AGRM to 'RP and G-AGRR to 'RT, but the remaining 11 production Viking 498s started normal services with BEA.

BEA's 11 Viking 498s were, not surprisingly, christened with names beginning with V. And if *Vagrant*, *Value*, *Vagabond* and *Valet* (G-AGRU to 'RW and G-AHOR) seem unconvincing, then *Valentine*, *Valerie*, *Valiant*, *Valkyrie*, *Valley*, *Valour* and *Vanessa* are more plausible (G-AHON, G-AHOP and G-AHOS to G-AHOW).

As well as Viking 498 Mk 1As, BEA also bought nine improved Viking 614 Mk 1s as *Vanguard*, *Vanity*, *Vantage*, *Varlet*, *Variety*, *Vassal*, *Vampire*, *Vandal* and *Vedette* (G-AHOX to 'OZ, and G-AHPA to 'PF). These aircraft had conventional all-metal stressed skin wings outboard of the engines and similarly constructed tail surfaces; control surfaces were fabric-covered. The geodetic wing centre section was retained on the Mk 1s, but they were skinned with unstressed Alclad metal instead of fabric.

Subsequent Vikings had the all-metal wings and tail surfaces fitted to the Mk 1, and most of the early production Mk 1As with fabric-covered geodetic wings and tail surfaces were modified with the Mk 1's all-metal items.

BEA's Vikings used Northolt Airport instead of Heathrow when they were introduced, and the company's first Viking service was made on 1 September 1946, when

G-AHOP *Valerie* flew to Copenhagen. Further services followed. Some temporary icing problems which arose in December 1946 were solved, and BEA's Vikings soon became familiar sights on European routes, gaining a reputation as comfortable, reliable and unremarkable 21-passenger airliners.

As with other piston-engine airliners, while the Viking's engines did not look unduly large from outside the aircraft, they blocked the view out from the passenger cabin. There was a tiny nautical-looking vent mounted on the nacelle, visible from the cabin looking for all the world like a ship's galley chimney. I never discovered what fluid it vented, and, quite recently, I found out that there was another one mounted on the other side of the nacelle.

Unusually for an airliner, the Viking's wings were about a third of the way up from the bottom of the fuselage. The main spar crossed the passenger cabin floor and a step was provided for passing over it. It must have been a nuisance for cabin staff to have to pass back and forth over the main spar, and jokes were made about BEA's Viking air hostesses having well-developed calf muscles as a result!

BEA also received 44 Viking 610 Mk 1Bs in 1947. These aircraft were 2 ft 4 in (0.71 m) longer than previous variants and could take 24 to 27 passengers – previous Vikings carried 21 passengers. A second-hand Mk 1B joined BEA as Viking 636 G-AJJN *Vulcan*, the former Vickers demonstrator which had already a 29,000 mile (46,660 km) return flight to New Zealand lasting from April to June 1947.

Cabin address systems were not normally fitted in airliners of those days, and the Viking was no exception. Well into the journey, when boredom had set in after the noise and drama of take-off had become just a treasured (or terrifying) memory, a hand-written note from the captain was passed from passenger to passenger, giving information such as speed, altitude, position, and the Viking's name, etc. If Paris could "be seen on the left" when the note was passed from the flight deck, then the city might still be visible when the note reached the final passenger, as the Viking bumbled along at 180 mph (290 km/h)!

Vikings were normally fitted with large propeller spinners, but they were sometimes removed, as I discovered after boarding BEA's G-AJBR *Virginia*, a 610 Mk 1B, in 1950 or thereabouts. Some years later, during the mid-fifties, I saw a Viking taxiing at Blackbushe with only one spinner, but I cannot remember if it flew like that.

A distinguished task for the Viking was its service on the Royal Flight, for which four Mk 1s were delivered. VL246 and VL247 were fitted out for King George VI and Queen Elizabeth (the late Queen Mother), respectively. The accommodation was divided into two saloons, each being provided with two forward and two rearward facing seats; an interesting touch was the fitting of a clock, altimeter and ASI in each saloon. VL245 was a staff transport and VL248 was taken on as a flying workshop; the staff Viking was delivered to Benson RAF on 12 August 1946 and the three others arrived in early 1947.

The Vikings' first assignment was the Royal Tour of South Africa, starting in March 1947, and the aircraft flew to South Africa in stages while the King, Queen and Princesses Elizabeth and Margaret went by sea from Portsmouth in the UK's last battleship, HMS *Vanguard*. Vickers gained good publicity from the Vikings' reliable performance during the tour, as well as from the *cachet* of being chosen for the Royal Flight. The aircraft were pensioned off from the Flight in April 1958.

Excluding the three prototypes, 163 Vikings were built. No other British medium-haul airliner had been built in such numbers up to that time, although the Viscount sold in much greater quantity later on. Apart from BEA, some of the Viking's operators included the Argentine Government, which took 20, Aer Lingus (7), Air India (9), Airwork (6), Central African Airways (5), DDL or Danish Air Lines (5), Hunting Air Travel (2), Indian National Airways (6), Iraqi Airways (2) and South African Airways (8).

Vikings were designed as short/medium haul airliners, but Central African Airways successfully flew Vikings on its long-haul service from London to Salisbury in Southern Rhodesia (now Harare in Zimbabwe). Flying in easy stages, the journey took four or five days, depending on route, and overnight stops were made. A former passenger from the mid 'fifties describes the in-flight nourishment as "not bad" and recalls that it was given out in blue metal lunch boxes which had to be returned afterwards.

Converted Viking 1Bs entered service with BEA on 12 October 1952 with passenger capacity increased to 36. Maximum take-off weight rose from the Mk 1's 34,000 lb (15,422 kg) to 36,712 lb (16,653 kg). Known as Admiral Class Vikings, these aircraft were rechristened, the first one being G-AIVL *Lord Hawke* (ex *Vigilant*) which had been converted after a terrorist bomb exploded in the WC over the English Channel on 13 April 1950. Captain I R Harvey later received the George Medal for getting the aircraft back to Northolt where, after an overshoot, he made a safe landing.

Despite the above updates, the Viking was becoming uncompetitive on first-line routes by 1952, and within two years BEA had withdrawn them from service. The surplus Vikings were sold to independent operators such as Autair, BKS, Eagle, Hunting Clan and Tradair, to name but some. Most of these Vikings changed hands more than once, serving in diminishing numbers until by 1970 they had practically all been withdrawn.

Until 1952 the Viking was the only post-war British medium-haul airliner in service. Although a fine and successful aircraft, it was the poor relation to more modern American airliners, and the Viking's inferiority to the Convair 240 in performance was manifest.

But the Viking was an interim airliner and was never intended to be a Convair. It was available when it was needed, it sold at home and overseas, saved us dollar expenditure on American aircraft, and was good enough to stay in service for over 20 years after production ended.

****

At some stage during WW2 it had become likely that victory over the Allies' two major opponents, Germany and Japan, was only a matter of time, and the UK would have to start planning for production of a post-war generation of airliners. We were a major producer of aircraft in those days, with vast experience of design and production amassed over the previous 40 years and it was natural that our post-war airliners would be British-designed, British-built and powered by British engines. The Brabazon Committee was formed to decide the

The prototype Viking, G-ACOK, first flew in June 1945   *B Robertson*

types of post-war airliners which might be needed, and the result of the Committee's second sitting, from 25 May 1943 to 12 November 1945, were detailed specifications for nine different types of airliner. Specifications for three short-haul aircraft led to the Vickers Viscount and Armstrong-Whitworth Apollo turboprop airliners, as well as the piston-engined Airspeed Ambassador, the latter first flying in 1947 - all of them were advanced machines which would not be ready for service for several years after WW2.

However, a machine for immediate post-war use was urgently needed, a requirement which the Brabazon Committee had not addressed. Therefore, the Viking was designed by Vickers-Armstrongs under Government sponsorship as a stop-gap airliner based on the Wellington bomber, which had made such a good name for itself during WW2. The twin-engined Viking was essentially a passenger-carrying fuselage married to Wellington wings and the Warwick V's tailplane, and powered by the Wellington's Bristol Hercules engines.

The Viking was designed as a short/medium-haul machine, in the same category as the obsolescent DC-3, but with more powerful engines and higher performance. Unlike its Wellington parent, which had a certain functional visual appeal, the Viking had a portly, if roomy, fuselage, which gave the Viking an unfortunate and foreshortened appearance, preventing the machine from being good looking from almost any angle. But if the Viking looked wrong, it defied the old adage that what looks right is right and it proved to be an excellent aircraft. The aircraft was thoroughly sorted before it first flew thanks to its proven Wellington origins, and the Viking sold in reasonable numbers not only in the UK, but also in export markets.

An early Viking with leading edge exhaust collector rings   *B Robertson*

The portly lines of one of the three prototype Vikings *Aeroplane*

The VC1 (Vickers Commercial 1) Viking was initially referred to as the Wellington Transport Aircraft by the Ministry of Aircraft Production. By late 1944, with the aircraft's gestation under way, the type was named the Viking, and, as a result of using existing Wellington components, the Viking's gestation period was considerably shortened. The prototype Viking, G-AKOK, one of three prototypes, first flew on 22 June 1945, just six weeks after the war in Europe had ended, in the hands of Capt J 'Mutt' Summers from Wisley Airfield, Surrey, near Vickers' Weybridge base. The Viking was the first post-war British medium-haul airliner to fly, and was powered by two 1,675 hp Bristol Hercules 130 fourteen-cylinder aircooled radials.

The new generation of post-war short/mediul-haul airliners of the late 'forties incorporated pressurised cabins, reversible-pitch propellers and nose-wheel undercarriages. However, the Viking had none of these up-to-date features, being a stop-gap airliner pending the introduction of more modern types. The unpressurised Viking was designed to fly at moderate altitudes, for which the single-speed superchargers of its Hercules 130s were adequate. The well-known Bristol leading-edge exhaust collector ring, so long a feature of Bristol radial engines and used in the Wellington, was exchanged for a more modern rear facing exhaust system in the prototype Viking, although some early Vikings were initially fitted with the older system. The Viking retained the fabric-covered wings of its Wellington parent, a dated feature not used on more modern British or US airliners. However, despite its dated design features, the Viking was designed to meet modern airworthiness requirements, in particular, the new ICAO standards for single-engined operation.

The prototype weighed 33,500 lb (15,196 kg) and cruised at about 200 mph (320 km/h); span and length of 89 ft 3 ins (27.20 m) and 62 ft 10 ins (19.15 m) were little different from the older DC-3's corresponding dimensions, but the Viking had 40 per cent more power than the Pratt & Whitney-engined DC-3. The prototype G-AGOK is shown at the head of

The second prototype Viking, G-AGOL, shows off its Wellington origins *Aeroplane*

4

The second prototype, G-AGOL, again   *Aeroplane*

page 3. This machine was ordered with the military serial TT194, which was changed for the civil registration G-AGOK in May 1945. G-AKOK had an innings of only about ten months as it made a forced landing on 23 April 1946 at Effingham, Surrey. It is just possible to see that the Viking in the head-on picture on page 3 has early leading edge exhaust collectors, so the aircraft shown may be the third prototype G-AGOM. This machine first flew on 19 November 1945, and was at the official naming ceremony of London Airport on 25 March 1946. G-AGOM was lent to the BOAC Development Flight at Hurn from 18 May to 3 June 1946, and, that year, it gave a demonstration at the Tollerton Air Display on 21 September, and then at White Waltham on the 29th for the Business Man's Air Show. The second prototype, G-AGOL, shown left and on the previous page, has the more modern rear exhaust system ultimately used on most Vikings; this machine was dismantled at RAF St Athan in 1958.

The Ministry of Aircraft Production placed an order for 50 Vikings on 5 April 1946 and the type received its Certificate of Airworthiness (CoA) on 24 April. It looked as though Railway Air Services (RAS) would be the first Viking operator. This operator had been formed in 1934 by the then British national flag carrier, Imperial Airways, and the four major privately-owned railway companies, names of which will strike chords with steam enthusiasts, namely the Great Western (GWR), London Midland and Scottish (LMS), Southern Railway (SR) and the London and North Eastern Railway (LNER), which, incidentally, took the world's speed record for steam of 126 mph on 3 July 1939 – a record that still stands and is unlikely to be challenged.

RAS ran an extensive internal route network in the UK during the 'thirties, and after WW2 planned to extend services to the Continent with, among other machines, Vikings. The firm's post-war fleet included such aircraft as the DC-3, Avro XIX (civil Anson), DH Dragon Rapide and, no less, some German JU52 tri-motors. But Clement Attlee's post-war Labour government created state-owned British European Airways in 1946 (now part of BA), which took over RAS on 1 February 1947, so the Vikings went, instead, to the new BEA.

Indian National Airways' VT-AZA with open hold doors   *Aeroplane*

Nineteen early production Vikings retained the Wellington-based geodetic fabric-covered wings of the prototype, but they had Hercules 630 engines giving 1,690 hp instead of the prototype's 1,675 hp Hercules 130s. These machines started work as Viking 498s (later designated 498 Mk 1A), the number reflected the tailoring of aircraft to meet customer's individual needs. G-AGON, the first production model, made its first flight on 23 March 1946, and started off life with the BOAC Development Flight at Hurn, gaining its CoA on 10 May. It

A Viking in early BEA livery, and with the early exhaust system *B Robertson*

was transferred to BEA on 2 May 1947 for crew training, and then in August it went to the Ministry of Supply as VW214, and then back to civil use in 1954 as G-AGON with Eagle Aircraft Services operating from Blackbushe Airport in Surrey, this Viking's first service carrying passengers. There followed a spell with BKS, and G-AGON was then withdrawn from service and dismantled in 1955. The next seven Viking 498s, G-AGRM to 'RP and G-AGRR to 'RT had assorted careers. At the end of its service, G-AGRM had an undignified *finale* in January 1955 when used to demonstrate an escape tool comprising a large mechanical saw! G-AGRN met a similarly sad ending used by the RAF School of fire-fighting. G-AGRO's career only lasted about three years before its registration was cancelled in February 1948, after which this Viking was used as a source of spare parts!

The remaining 11 Viking 498s entered service in what is probably the Viking's best-remembered role, when they joined BEA for normal services in 1946 as G-AGRU to 'RW, G-AHON, 'OP, and G-AHOR to 'OW, faithfully serving through several subsequent changes of ownership, some until the early 'sixties, by which time they were well and truly obsolete. These BEA machines were all christened with names starting, appropriately, with V – *Vagrant, Value, Vagabond, Valentine, Valerie, Valet, Valiant, Valkyrie, Valley, Valour* and *Vanessa*. Some of these names seem oddly chosen, and while, for instance, *Valentine, Valerie* and *Vanessa* are much improved, *Vagabond* and *Vagrant* sound rather tongue-in-cheek, and *Value* sounds like a supermarket!

As well as taking delivery of Viking 498s with their fabric-covered wings and tail surfaces, BEA also took nine 614 Mk 1s as G-AHOX to 'OZ, and G-AHPA to 'PF, again with 'V' names *Vanguard, Vanity, Vantage, Varlet, Variety, Vassal, Vampire, Vandal* and *Vedette*. The 614 Mk 1s broke away from the fabric-covered wings/tail, and were more up to date

G-AGRW Vagabond was a BEA Viking 498 Mk 1A – note the early type of exhaust system *Aeroplane*

The Viking 610 Mk 1B was longer than the original aircraft   *B Robertson*

with conventional all-metal stressed skin wings in keeping with other contemporary airliners. However the centre wing sections inboard of the engines retained the geodetic wing structure of earlier aircraft, with an unstressed Alclad metal surface instead of fabric used on earlier aircraft. Fabric-covered control surfaces were retained. All subsequent Vikings (Mk 1Bs) had these structural features and most of the early production models (498 Mk 1As), with fabric-covered geodetic wings and tail surfaces, were upgraded to Mk 1 standards with the later stressed skin structure.

BEA's Vikings used Northolt, a former wartime military airfield, rather than Heathrow when the Vikings were introduced. The firm's inaugural Viking service was made on 1 September 1946 when Viking 498 G-AHOP *Valerie* flew from Northolt to Copenhagen (Capt L G James), followed by services to Stavanger, Oslo and Amsterdam. Only a few months after entering service, BEA's Viking Mk 1s encountered icing on the leading edges of their metal tail planes in winter conditions, causing elevator overbalance. Problems were eventually cured by modifying the elevators and increasing the flow rate of de-icing fluid over the tail plane leading edge, and Vikings went back to work with a clean bill of health in April 1947.

It is interesting to note the de-icing method used on the Viking, metering de-icing fluid to the affected area. Means of de-icing on some other aircraft included leading-edge pulsating de-icer boots to dislodge the ice (e.g. Lockheed

The Viking was a roomy aircraft, with three-abreast seating. Note the open luggage racks   *Aeroplane*

The Queen disembarks from VL246, one of four 623 Mk 1s allocated to the Royal Flight *B Robertson*

Constellation, Handley-Page Hermes), and thermal means which, in the DC-6 and Ambassador involved passing warm air through leading edge ducting heated by petrol-fired heaters – the latter led to early problems with the DC-6 and a tragic crash after an in-flight fire; the DC-6 was grounded while the problem was identified and cured.

Apart from icing problems, the Viking was relatively trouble-free, having been developed from the proven Wellington bomber, and BEA expanded its Viking services within Europe. BEA received 44 Viking Mk 610 Mk 1Bs, starting services with them in 1947. The Mk 1Bs were 2 ft 4 in (0.71 m) longer than earlier aircraft so they looked a little less rotund as a result. Passenger capacity was increased from 21 to 24 (later 27), and names beginning with V were used, the aircraft being G-AHPK to 'PP, 'PR, 'PS, G-AIVB to 'VP, G-AJBM to 'BP, 'BR to 'BY, G-AJCA, 'CD, 'CE, 'DI to 'DL, 'BG, and 'BH. Examples of their names included *Vigilant*, *Veracity*, *Verdant*, *Ventnor*, *Verity* etc. *Venus* was an inappropriate name for the portly Viking, but *Vimy* was reminiscent of the famous Vickers aircraft of around 30 years before, an example of which, in the hands of Alcock and Brown, made the first non-stop Atlantic crossing in 1919.

Royal Flight Viking VL246, again, with flags deployed *M J Hooks*

8

Royal Flight Viking VL248 was fitted out as a flying workshop   *B Robertson*

A second-hand Viking Mk 1B 636 joined BEA as G-AJJN. This Viking first flew on 6 April 1947 and was registered to its manufacturer, Vickers, as a demonstrator, as shown in the bottom picture on page 10. This machine flew to Auckland in 1947 on a demonstration trip, leaving Hurn on 13 April on what was an ambitious two week flight for a short/medium-haul twin, albeit made in stages via Marignane, Malta, Cairo, Basra, Karachi, Delhi, Calcutta, Rangoon, Penang, Singapore, Surabaya, Darwin, Cloncurry, Brisbane and Sydney! G-AJJN arrived in Auckland on 28 April. After demonstration flying in New Zealand, the much-travelled Viking set off for home leaving Auckland on 12 May 1947, arriving safely after a round trip of over 29,000 miles (46,660 km). Despite this impressive flight which amounted to around 150 hours of flying time, no Vikings were sold in New Zealand. G-AJJN was converted to a 610 and sold to BEA, delivered on 13 December 1949 as *Vulcan*. This machine enjoyed a good innings with various owners and ended up with Channel Airways in the Autumn of its years, being withdrawn on 18 February 1963 by which time the Viking was obsolete in an age of jetliners.

The Viking's contemporaries were more up-to-date, and it was old-fashioned for a post-war medium-haul airliner, with its tailwheel undercarriage, lack of pressurisation, and its absence of reversible-pitch propellers. The type was having to compete with the much more modern Covair 240, the latter machine having a tricycle undercarriage, pressurised cabin,

Royal Flight Viking VL246 was tastefully fitted out for King George VI   *B Robertson*

9

A Royal Flight Viking, possibly on the 1947 South African Royal Tour   *M J Hooks*

reversible-pitch propellers and much higher performance, enabling it to manage the flight between Heathrow and Geneva in around two hours. The Viking took three hours to fly between Northolt and Geneva. In addition, the Convair carried 40 passengers as opposed to the Viking 1B's 24/27.

I was acutely conscious of the Viking's inferiority to the Convair 240, but this was not a criticism of the Viking or of those who designed it, because the Viking was hastily conceived as stop-gap airliner for use until more modern types could be introduced. Despite the Viking's stop-gap nature, it was a sound, reliable aircraft and it served BEA well until the arrival of more modern types (Elizabethan and Viscount). Also, Convairs and Vikings were built in roughly equal numbers for civil operators, so the Viking clearly had features demanded by customers. Even if BEA had eyed the Convair with envy while it waited to take delivery of the Viking's more modern successors, it would have been inconceivable in those days for BEA to buy American Convairs instead of Vikings built in the UK. BEA became the Viking's principal operator, and BEA's machines became common sights on Europe's air routes, so common, indeed, that one hardly bothered to look up when the familiar, rough noise of twin Hercules engines heralded a Viking flying overhead.

I still associate Vikings with their Northolt home base. The picture on the right shows a typical group of BEA Vikings, almost certainly at Northolt, in their early BEA livery before Vikings were given the fashionable white cabin tops above the windows, which were said to keep cabin interiors cool. This picture shows the Viking's rotund shape and also shows how the view of the forward passengers is obscured by the bulky engine nacelles. Indeed this was a characteristic of propeller-driven airliners, a notable exception being the Viking's superb successor, the turboprop Viscount, and it was not until the advent of jetliners that the view for air passengers was improved. The Viking's wings were about a third of the way up from the bottom of the fuselage, which was unusual for an airliner, and, as a result, the main spar crossed the passenger cabin. The intrusive spar was neatly covered by a carpeted step, to be negotiated by cabin staff carrying trays which, in turbulent conditions must have led to a few near misses! It was said that BEA's stewardesses could be recognised by their

Vickers' demonstrator 636 Mk 1B flew to New Zealand and back in 1947   *B Robertson*

well-developed calf muscles thanks to this step!

With only 21 passengers, and three-abreast seating divided by an aisle, the Viking was "cosy", and would have seemed like a minibus to present day travellers used to even relatively small airliners carrying over 100 passengers. The picture at the bottom of page 7 shows that all is snug and happy aboard a BEA Viking possibly flying between European cities. When this photo was taken, far fewer people travelled by air, but it was also a time of rapid expansion of air travel

10

thanks to technical advances, many of which had been developed in the hard school of the recently-ended WW2. As an example of this, the Hercules engine gave 1,375 hp in 1940, but power had risen to 1,690 hp from the Viking's Herc 630 series six or seven years later, and at about that time an even more powerful version of the Hercules was giving over 2,000 hp.

I made numerous flights with BEA in Vikings between Northolt and Geneva during the late 'forties and early 'fifties, and I grew to like the aircraft. It gave the impression of bumbling friendliness. The cabin attendant was usually

A group of Vikings, possibly at Northolt, showing G-AJJN now with BEA *M J Hooks*

female and known as an air hostess, while male cabin staff were referred to as stewards – a term no doubt borrowed from passenger ships. The Viking had a portly, roomy, fuselage, and the nacelles of the two Bristol Hercules engines looked

G-AIXR started off with Airwork in 1947, and, after changes of ownership, was withdrawn in 1963 *M J Hooks*

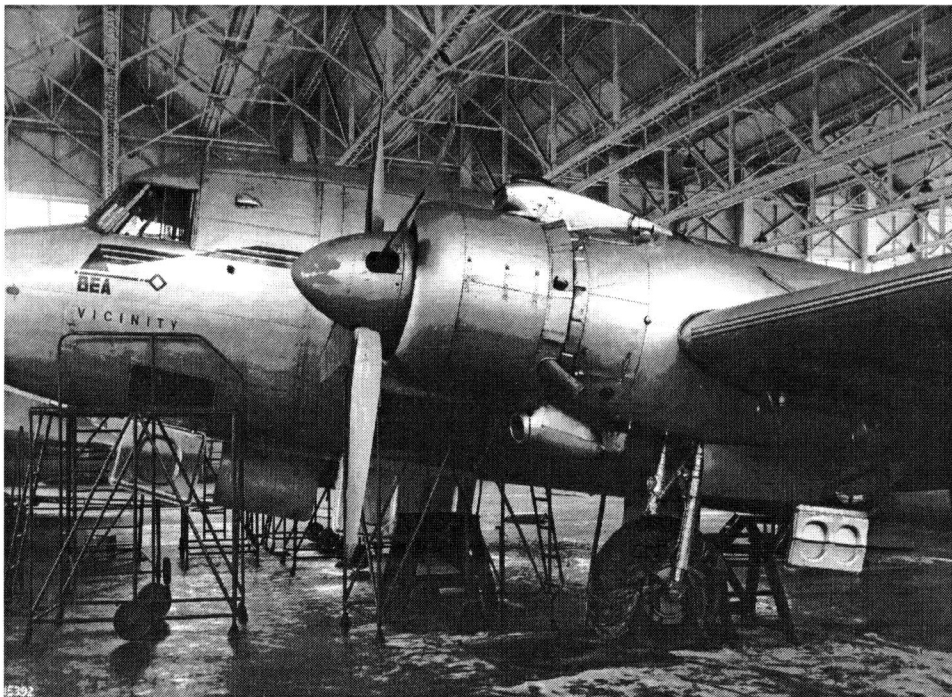

BEA's G-AIVH 610 Mk 1B *Vicinity* became Admiral Class *Lord Howe* *Aeroplane*

enormous from the passenger cabin, and the aim was to try to secure a seat behind the wing trailing edge in order to get a decent view – seats were not allocated in those days, and the first passenger to board could choose the best seat.

Pre-take-off engine run-up was part of the routine of piston-engined flight, to check the correct functioning of the ignition system (spark ignition was normal, diesel engines were not used on aircraft), propeller pitch control, etc. The run up was a dramatic, noisy time, and on one occasion I happened to look back out of the cabin window and could see the tailplane vibrating strongly, buffeted by the propeller slipstream from the two powerful Hercs. Sometimes it's best not to know too much of what goes on, and I looked away, wondering how the tailplane managed to stand up to this sort of hammering.

Then there was the exciting and noisy drama of take-off, with both Hercs giving full power for the brief time of take-off and initial climb. As with other piston-engines, both Hercs sounded stressed at full power, and it was a relief when they were eased back to climb power. Engine failure with a fully-loaded Viking at take-off would almost certainly have meant disaster, as the Viking's ability to climb away on one engine seemed to be largely theoretical. I was once told at a BEA check-in desk not to worry about engine failure as the Hercs were very reliable (true) and, in any case, the Viking could

Possibly the Vickers demonstrator Viking G-AJJN which flew to New Zealand and back *Aeroplane*

Viking 620 Mk 1 LV XEN was delivered to the Argentine Government in July 1946 *Aeroplane*

climb at 1,000 ft per minute on one engine - definitely not true – this would have needed the services of both engines at full load!

In all my years of flying in piston-engined aircraft, I never once experienced an engine failure. But I did have one hairy moment during the summer of 1949 in a Viking. We were coming in to land at Geneva one very hot day, three hours out from Northolt. The touchdown was normal, then suddenly all hell broke loose as the Viking veered off the runway to starboard at high speed, bumping along the grass at 80 mph (129 km/h) completely out of control, flanked by two very hot engines and enough fuel for a diversion. The propellers stopped turning almost immediately as the skipper switched off the engines to reduce the fire risk in case of landing gear collapse, and on we bumped, propellers conspicuously still, slowing down more or less in a straight line. We eventually came to a halt, slewing round as we did so. Luckily the undercarriage held together, and we all got out about a mile from the terminal buildings, standing round the aircraft awaiting rescue by a coach. It turned out that a tyre had burst on landing. I took the opportunity of having a good look at the Viking while we waited, and went under the wheel well, feeling the heat from the engine. A near miss if ever there was one. Had the landing gear collapsed, the legs might have punctured the saddle tanks in the engine nacelles behind the engines, and the probable result of that needs little imagination.

A pleasing photograph, showing the Viking's debt to the Wellington *B Robertson*

The splendid picture on page 12 shows Viking Mk 1B 610 G-AIVH *Vicinity* in a hangar at Northolt. This was the view that passengers about to embark sometimes had of the Viking as they walked out to the aircraft from the departure lounge, a squat burly-looking aircraft which gave the impression of dependability. The features of the port Hercules engine are shown to good advantage. The forward-

G-AHPN _Ventnor_ at Geneva's Cointrin Airport, framed by the Salève mountain _Aeroplane_

facing carburettor air intake sits atop the nacelle, while the oil cooler is under it. A vestigial exhaust pipe peeps out from behind the engine cowling.

The bulky nacelle, behind the engine cowling, houses the undercarriage when retracted. The undercarriage doors, which close after retraction to cover the gap, can also be seen. On modern airliners, the doors close to cover the void left when the undercarriage is down, and, although some aircraft had this refinement in the Viking's day, most did not, and the Viking was no exception. The circumferential cooling air exit behind the engine cowling gave passengers a good view of the exhaust collector ring, which glowed red hot at night, much to the concern of nervous occupants! Lastly, the propeller spinner gave the engine a streamlined look, which was lacking on many American airliners, an exception to this being the beautifully streamlined Constellation. Although Vikings were normally fitted with spinners, they were sometimes removed, as I discovered after boarding G-AJBR _Virginia_, a BEA 610 Mk 1B, in 1950 or thereabouts. Some years later in 1956/7, I saw a Viking at Blackbushe with only one spinner, whether or not it flew in this condition I cannot remember, but it was certainly taxiing.

The Hercules radial was one of the few aero engines fitted with sleeve-valves, a feature which cost Bristol dear during the 'thirties when the firm was developing sleeve-valve engines and trying to make them work properly, under the direction of Roy Fedden (later Sir Roy). He became a well-known designer of aircooled radials pre-WW2 and one of his hallmarks was four-valve cylinder heads, which were simple enough to provide on his single-row engines, but more complex on two-row engines. So, for the two-row Hercules, Fedden chose sleeve valves instead of conventional poppet valves. Severe sleeve-valve development problems were resolved in time for Herc production for WW2. But the Hercules might have given good results with poppet valves and two valve heads, which worked well on the excellent two-row engines built by both Pratt and Whitney and Wright.

Two Rolls-Royce Nene turbojets gave the Viking real performance! _M J Hooks_

The Hercules was a great engine, possibly despite its sleeve valves rather than because of them, and in 1951 a Viking's Hercules 634, built entirely of pooled components from Vikings operated by Airwork and BEA, many of which had already run over 3,000 hrs i.e. over 600,000 miles (965,000 km), underwent a 100-hour civil type test. The Herc performed faultlessly, and the components, when the

14

Used by the RAF for transport and training, the Valetta was based on the Viking   *B Robertson*

engine was stripped down, were well within limits. A Herculean performance! Not long afterwards, the overhaul life of the Hercules in Vikings was extended to 1,250 hours, no less than 250,000 miles (402,000 km)!

During my numerous Viking flights between Northolt and Geneva, I clearly remember some of the details even now over half a century later. A flight between Northolt and Geneva meant spending three hours flanked by the two rumbling Hercules. It never occurred to me that they would do anything other than just carry on running until switch-off at the other end. As the picture on page 7 shows, some of the rows of seats faced one another, and passengers occupying facing rows, total strangers at the start of the flight, sometimes struck up conversations and had become old friends by touchdown. On one occasion, when the air hostess brought lunch round on the usual plastic trays, the passenger opposite me asked if he could swap his apple for my roll, as apples disagreed with him. Looking at my crisp roll and the inviting pat of butter on the tray beside it, I reluctantly agreed – young and impressionable as I was at the age of nine.

On one flight, I discovered, to my horror, that I had lost my passport, and so I spent the rest of the flight agonising over

Loading a carriage-mounted gun through the wide doors of a Valetta   *Aeroplane*

my reception in Geneva without a passport, imagining that I would be banished back to Northolt on the next return flight. Salvation arrived towards the end of the journey when the air hostess came up and gave me my "lost" passport, which she had taken from me for the duration of the flight for safe keeping. Quite how she got hold of it, I still cannot remember.

On another BEA flight, this time from Geneva to Northolt, the steward (for some reason we never called them air hosts!) came up and asked me to go and sit with a young lad of about my age who was

15

A glider-towing Valetta was a very rare sight, as gliders passed out of use after WW2 *B Robertson*

in a very bad way, consumed with homesickness at the thought of leaving Geneva and coming to England. Not wanting to get involved with a weeping contemporary, I declined, much to the steward's annoyance who was left to console this fellow youngster.

The Viking's status as the poor relation compared to the modern American airliners which then dominated the world's air routes was brought home to me on a BEA Viking flight. I suspect this flight may have been from Heathrow. We stopped in the holding area near the mouth of the runway to carry out the pre-take off engine run up. There was a TWA or BOAC Connie ahead of us doing the same thing, and as we were parked slightly askew I had a good view of this magnificent American running up its four Wright Duplex Cyclone engines. The Connie towered above the much smaller Viking, its shapely form so much more attractive than the Viking's appearance. I looked at the Connie as, engine checks complete, it slowly moved onto the runway and swung round for take-off, and I could clearly hear the roar of its mighty 18-cylinder engines from within the Viking's sound-proofed cabin as the Connie started its take-off run. I felt very small in 'my' Viking!

Like other airliners of its time the Viking had no cabin address system, even though the technology was undoubtedly available then, so there were no piped music or announcements about the forthcoming flight. Indeed I do not even remember cabin staff showing us what do to do during an emergency or how to use our life jackets, although the latter were provided. We were just expected to read the literature and make sure that we were briefed. Cabin staff offered barley sugar and chewing gum before take-off, allegedly to protect ears from discomfort during the climb, but possibly just to calm the fearful. I never discovered which, but it was a nice welcoming touch which would seem odd today. Cotton wool, I believe, was also offered for ears. These goodies were served from

The Valetta prototype first flew on 30 June 1947 as a C Mk 1 *Aeroplane*

16

Valetta C Mk 1 VL263 was used for paratrooping trials in 1948   *Aeroplane*

a tray brought round by the cabin attendant.

Then, as now, seat belts were provided and we were expected by cabin staff to use them. Large brown paper bags were also provided for those suffering from airsickness, and some of us needed no encouragement to use them! In the absence of an on-board PA system, a written note from a message pad was passed during the journey from the flight deck, giving details of the flight, e.g. speed, height, the Viking's name, and other details, such as position, e.g. "we are passing Paris to our left". The note was passed from passenger to passenger and we were expected to read it quickly and then pass it on before position information became out of date.

But this was rarely a problem as the Viking flew very sedately. The Viking's "brochure" cruising speed was 210 mph (338 km/h), but most of my flights on Vikings were well below this, a typical figure being about 180 mph (290 km/h), which seemed slow even over half a century ago. Thanks to its unpressurised cabin, the Viking flew at about 8,000 ft (2,440 m). As well as *Virginia*, already mentioned, I flew on a Viking whose handwritten name looked like *Vocant*. But, I later discovered that there was no such aircraft! A three-hour flight in a Viking, and other piston airliners, always left me

Valetta C Mk 1 VW141 shows the type's cockpit roof glazing, absent from its Viking sire   *Aeroplane*

Prototype Valetta C Mk 1 VL249 - probably a display of new types   *M J Hooks*

tired and jaded at the end of the flight. I think this may have been due to the noise and vibration which is absent from turbine engines. You had to raise your voice to talk to people in piston-engined airliners.

When the Viking was introduced, the UK had a large home grown manufacturing industry, and industry in general was told to "export or die". Allocations of steel to the motor industry, for instance, were made on condition that vehicles would be exported.

I don't know if this carrot and stick approach was applied to our aircraft industry, but a number of Vikings were exported and some of Vickers' export customers receiving Vikings included the Argentine Government which took 20 aircraft, Aer Lingus (7), Air India (9), Central African Airways (5), DDL or Danish Airlines (5), Indian National Airways (6), Iraqi Airways (2) and South African Airways (8). Aside from BEA, British customers included Airwork which took six machines, and Hunting Air Travel (2).

The Viking was a short/medium haul aircraft, but, reminiscent of G-AJJN's 29,000 mile (46,660 km) round trip to New Zealand, Central African Airways worked its long-haul route connecting London and Harare (then Salisbury) with Vikings. The journey was made in stages as the Viking lacked the range to make the flight non-stop, and the whole trip took four to five days, depending on route, with overnight stops. There is, of course, no reason why a short-haul aircraft should not be used for long-haul flights if made in stages, but several days spent on a Viking would be regarded as quite an ordeal by today's air travellers! A former passenger who used this African service during the mid 'fifties describes the in-flight meals as "not bad", and recalls that food was served in returnable blue metal lunch boxes! I certainly remember that BEA's in-flight lunches aboard their Vikings were good, despite the general post-war economic austerity of the time which resulted in food rationing until the early 'fifties.

The King's Flight was disbanded during WW2, but it was decided to reform it post-war. The question arose as to the type and number of aircraft to be used. With our large and experienced aircraft industry, and with national attitudes of the time, there can have been little doubt that a British aircraft should be used and, initially, three Vikings were to be allocated. In the event four Viking Mk 1s were specified, specially fitted out for the purpose, each with a flight deck crew of four comprising pilot, second pilot, navigator and radio officer. King George VI and Queen Elizabeth (the late Queen Mother)

The Nene-powered Viking, looking unexpectedly well-proportioned here   *M J Hooks*

flew separately, in VL246 and VL247, respectively. Both these Vikings were tastefully fitted out and, in each aircraft, the royal accommodation was divided into two saloons, each with four specially designed seats, adjustable and stressed to 25g. Two of these seats faced aft and the other two faced forward.

There was a steward's compartment and WC at the rear, and a wardrobe between both saloons. VL245 was a staff transport with an internal layout similar to that of a standard Viking airliner, while VL248 was fitted out as a maintenance

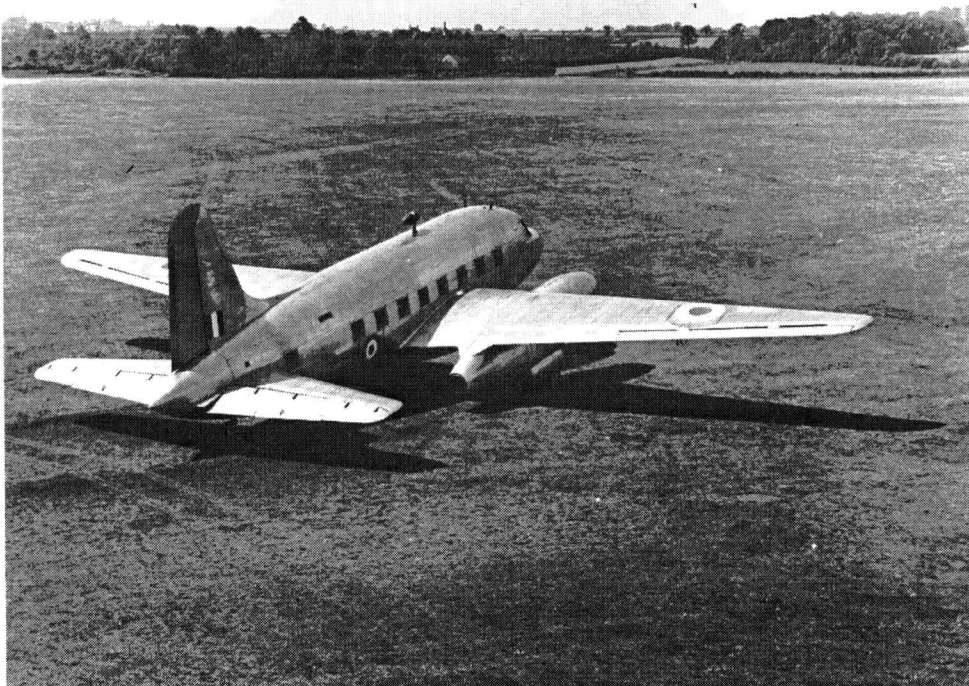

The Nene-Viking averaged 384 mph from London to Paris on 25 July 1948   *Aeroplane*

workshop. The staff Viking was delivered first out of the four royal machines, in August 1946, being the least modified of the four while the remaining three Vikings came in early 1947.

The Royal Vikings' first engagement was the Royal Tour of South Africa starting in early 1947, and the four aircraft flew to South Africa in stages to their tour base, Brooklyn Air Station near Capetown. Meanwhile, the King, Queen, Princess Elizabeth (now the Queen), and the late Princess Margaret went by sea leaving Portsmouth on 1 February 1947 in the UK's latest and last battleship HMS *Vanguard*, a ship which Princess Elizabeth had christened when it was launched in 1944. The Vikings were used to fly the Royal Family to their engagements during the Tour, clocking up a high mileage during which the machines performed well, gaining valuable publicity for Vickers, helped by the seal of approval gained from being selected for the Royal Flight. Not long afterwards, eight Viking Mk 1Bs were ordered by South African Airways.

The Royal Staff Transport Viking VL245 had a mishap in Scotland on 2 September 1947, due to engine problems just after take off, and the aircraft was damaged after landing in a field and hitting a stone wall. The King's Viking VL246 was sold in August 1958 and entered civil service as G-APOP, serving until the mid-sixties. The Queen's aircraft was also sold into civil service in August 1958, and made its final flight during the sixties. The workshop machine VL 248 was sold on in May 1955, and after civil use, which included service as a personal transport, was written off in an accident in 1964 in Mexico. With hindsight, it seems a pity that one of these ex-Royal Vikings was not saved for preservation for static display.

Compare the twin mainwheels on the Nene-powered Viking with the standard Viking gear on page 12   *Aeroplane*

19

Valetta C Mk 1 WJ491 served with A&AEE at Boscombe Down 1963 to '72 *M J Hooks*

The UK became a world leader in aircraft gas turbines at an early stage in their development, with several British firms involved in their production by the late 'forties, notably Rolls-Royce who, in 1944, had produced the Nene turbojet, the world's most powerful aero-engine at that time (and deliberately designed to be so) with a then very high thrust of 5,000 lb (2,268 kg). The UK capitalised on its gas turbine lead post-war, introducing the word's first jetliner to enter regular airline service, the de Havilland Comet, and the turboprop Viscount which became our most successful airliner and a major export earner – as would the Comet have been, but for a series of crashes which grounded the machine while the fault was cured, enabling the Americans to take our jetliner lead.

The British, it seemed, were willing to fit gas turbines to anything that would fly, and Viking 618 G-AJPH had its Hercules engines replaced by a couple of Roll-Royce Nenes slung under the wings, in which form the now-high speed Viking first flew on 6 April 1948 as the world's most unlikely jet transport aircraft. The extra loading resulting from the Nene's increased power was met with thicker skinning on wings and tail surfaces, as well as metal covered elevators, and a twin-wheel undercarriage each side. The Nene-Viking was essentially a research aircraft rather than a functioning transport, but it demonstrated its high performance on 25 July 1948 by flying from Heathrow to Paris in just over 34 minutes at 384 mph (618 km/h) – a piston engined Viking cruised at little more than half this speed! All good things must come to an end, and the Nenes were exchanged in 1954 for the aircraft's normal Hercules to make a Viking 1B. This unusual Viking ended its life with its fuselage being dumped in a gravel pit in 1961. The Nene Viking is shown on previous pages, and the picture on page 19 shows the twin wheel undercarriage needed to cope with higher landing weights and speeds of the jet-powered machine.

Converted Viking 1Bs entered service with BEA on 12 October 1952, with passenger capacity increased to 36 and a rise in maximum take-off weight to 36,712 lb (16,653 kg). Known as the Admiral Class, the Vikings were re-christened accordingly and the first example was G-AIVL *Lord Hawke* (ex-*Vigilant*). Before conversion, this machine demonstrated the Viking's robust construction on 13 April 1950 when a terrorist bomb planted in the WC exploded, seriously injuring the air hostess and badly damaging the Viking's rear structure. The Viking was heading for Paris and Captain Harvey turned back to Northolt, landing safely without loss of life, and earning a well-deserved George Medal. Fortunately the air hostess recovered. The aircraft was repaired and rebuilt as the first member of the Admiral Class, going back into service on 4 October 1950. BEA disposed of the aircraft in April 1955 and it was eventually broken up at Heathrow in 1961.

The Viking was considered to be a safe and reliable aircraft during its time, but, apart from the terrorist bomb on G-AIVL, there were inevitable mishaps, and between 1945 and 1965 a number of aircraft were written off due to accidents - not all of them involving loss of life or injury. My own experience, already recounted, of veering off the runway after landing due to tyre failure, happened on at least two other occasions (not to me) and the undercarriage collapsed each time although fortunately without fire. One such incident happened at New Delhi on 8 October 1948 to Indian National Airways' Viking 604 Mk 1B VT-CEJ *Ganges*, on a flight from New Delhi to Calcutta with a crew of 4 and 19 passengers. All on board survived.

On another occasion Eagle Aviation's Viking 635 Mk 1B G-AMGG suffered a starboard tyre failure on landing at Agadir, Morocco, with a crew of 4 and 32 passengers. As with the previous incident, all occupants survived. G-AMGG, incidentally, started off as South African Airways' ZS-BNE *Simonsberg* and was delivered on 31 July 1947. The aircraft was sold to BEA in November 1950 and became Admiral Class G-AMGG *Sir Robert Alder*, one of eight Vikings sold to BEA by SAA. After serving five years with BEA, G-AMGG was sold on to Eagle. Other Viking accidents were ascribed, variously, to engine failure, poor weather, crew error, etc. BEA lost six of its machines, none of them due to engine failure, for which brief details are listed below:

6 January 1948, Viking 610 Mk 1B G-AHPK *Veracity*. Crashed at Ruislip on the approach to Northolt in the dark, ex Glasgow. All survived except the pilot.

Former SAA Viking ZS-BNE *Simonsberg* became BEA's G-AMGG Admiral Class *Sir Robert Calder*   M J Hooks

5 April 1948 Viking 610 Mk 1B G-AIVP *Vimy*. Collided with a Russian warplane on the approach to Gatow (Berlin) All 14 on board perished, as did the Russian pilot.

21 April 1948 Viking 610 Mk 1B G-AIVE *Vestal*. Crashed into the Irish Law mountain on the approach to Renfrew (Glasgow), ex Northolt. All 20 on board survived.

31 October 1950 Viking 610 Mk 1B G-AHPN *Ventnor*. Crashed at Heathrow on overshoot ex Paris. One passenger and the air hostess survived.

5 January 1953 Viking 610 Mk 1B Admiral Class G-AJDL *Lord St Vincent*. Crashed at Nutts Corner (Belfast) in the dark ex Northolt. Eight survivors; 27 occupants died.

12 August 1953 Viking 610 Mk 1B Admiral Class G-AIVG *Sir George Rooke*. Tyre burst on take-off at Le Bourget (Paris). All on board survived.

BEA was by far the largest Viking operator, and, of the 163 production machines built, BEA operated over 60. So, relative to passenger-miles flown by BEA's Vikings over the years, the list above highlights the airline's excellent safety record with its Vikings, as well as the reliability of the aircraft's Bristol Hercules engines. Although Viking 616 Mk 1B VP-YEY *Shangani*, one of CAA's machines, disintegrated in flight on its way from Blantyre (Malawi) to Dar-es-Salaam in 1953 during a sudden gust of wind, the Viking was considered to be a rugged and soundly engineered aircraft and structural weakness was definitely not one of its characteristics.

During the piston-engined era, the characteristics that made airliners useful to civil operators were also attractive to the military, and, in the USA, military versions were produced of the Convair twins, Douglas DC-4 and DC-6, as well as the Lockheed Constellation and other types. Nowadays, more specialist machines are used as military transports than converted airliners. The practice of developing variants of airliners for military use was also pursued in the UK, notably in the case of the Viking.

A development of the Viking 1B for use as a military transport was produced, known as the Valetta C Mk 1, initially aimed at replacing the RAF's Dakotas. The aircraft had to be suitable for transporting military equipment such as vehicles, guns, supply containers and general items, as well as troops and paratroops. The aircraft also had to be suitable for use as an air ambulance and supply dropping. The Valetta was given a stronger cabin floor than the Viking 1B, and a large double door in the port side of the rear fuselage for loading bulky items, as shown at the bottom of page 15. A smaller door was incorporated with the double door for personnel access and paratroop entry, which is shown on page 17. The photo on page 17 also shows how the Viking's pointed rear fuselage cone has been removed from the Valetta, making a rather unsightly result. Indeed the sawn off rear fuselage was a feature of Valettas except for the C Mk 2, which had the Viking's more elegant cone.

BEA's G-AHPL V*erdant* is attended to at Rome, while a BEA Viscount takes off *Aeroplane*

There were lashing points in the cabin for securing cargo, and other items were available to suit the Valetta's various roles, including loading winch, floor mounted roller runways to allow positioning of cargo, stretchers, oxygen cylinders, seats, etc. The pantomime on page 15 in which several strong men are trying to load a mobile gun into the Valetta's roomy fuselage seems to be entirely manual, despite the Valetta's loading winch!

Not surprisingly, the Valetta was heavier than its Viking 1B parent, by 2,500 lb (1,134 kg), and so the Valetta was given more powerful engines in the form of 1,980 hp Hercules 230s. These were military engines which, like the Viking's Herc 234s, had single-speed superchargers, giving the Valetta a generous 17 per cent more power than the Viking to cover a 7.4 per cent weight increase.

Airwork took delivery of Viking 1B G-AIXR in May 1947 *M J Hooks*

Independent airlines, including Hunting-Clan, bought Vikings once owned by BEA, etc   *Aeroplane*

The differences between the Viking's 1,690 hp Hercules 634 and the Valetta's 1,980 hp Herc 230 demonstrate how engine manufacturers then, as now, extract ever more power from engines over time. Both powers are take-off ratings, and the 230's power increase of 17 per cent meant strengthening the engine, resulting in greater weight.

The Viking's Hercules 634 weighed 1,945 lb (882 kg), while the Valetta's Herc 230 weighed in at an even heftier 2,115 lbs (959 kg), i.e. about 9 per cent giving the Valetta's engine an 8 per cent better power to weight ratio – such is development. All Herc variants had 38.7 litres, massive by road vehicle standards, but typical for a large piston engine.

Autair's Viking Mk 1B G-AHPL was once BEA's Admiral Class *Lord Anson*   *Aeroplane*

In the roomy fuselage of a Varsity; note the side-by-side flight deck crew   *B Robertson*

The Hercules' superchargers were normal fitments for this class of engine. As both the 230 and 634 Hercs gave their maximum power at 2,800 rpm, then I assume that Bristol obtained the Valetta's power increase by increasing the boost - a time-honoured method of increasing the power of supercharged engines. Both the Viking and Valetta were unpressurised and therefore essentially moderate altitude aircraft, so single-speed supercharges gave the required boost. Incidentally, high-flying Hercs needed two-speed superchargers, as in the Herc 763s fitted to the Hermes airliner, which was pressurised and flew at up to 20,000 ft (6,096 m).

The prototype Varsity first flew from Wisley as VX828 on 17 July 1949   *M J Hooks*

By then end of WW2 there was a realisation that airliners should be able to fly safely with a failed engine, and the Viking was designed to meet the new International Civil Aviation Authority (ICAO) standards for single-engine operation and, indeed the Viking developed a reputation for good single-engine flight characteristics. The ability to perform satisfactorily on one engine at moderate weights was one thing, and the Airspeed Ambassador impressed by taking off on one engine at the 1948 Farnborough Air Display, but as weight increased a twin-engined airliner's single-engine performance

24

became less sprightly and when flying at maximum weight (i.e. with a full load of passengers and baggage) it was evident from accident records that post-war twins, even though they met the ICAO requirement, were hard put maintain height on one engine at normal operating weights.

On 8 May 1951, G-AHPD, a Viking 639 Mk1 operated by Hunting Air Travel, had problems with its port engine just after take off from Bordeaux-Merignac bound for Bovingdon. The Viking was carrying 27 passengers, and, unable to maintain height even with the good engine running at full power, the aircraft made a forced landing at Beutre and was damaged beyond repair. It was found that the linkage to the propeller constant speed governor had come adrift due to a missing split pin.

Another engine-related incident involved G-AHPM of Eagle Aviation Ltd, formerly BEA's *Lord Rodney*, on a trooping flight from the UK to the Middle East in September 1953. The flight was made in stages, and the pre-take off engine run-up at Nice identified a faulty starboard magneto. French engineers changed the magneto and the flight continued to Malta. An hour out from Malta en route to El Adem, the starboard engine failed and, with its propeller feathered, the Viking headed back to Malta. The Viking's port engine struggled in a losing battle to maintain height, but fortunately the aircraft managed to reach Malta for a safe landing before running out of altitude. The problem turned out to be a ruptured boost capsule. With these two Viking stories in mind, I would be interested to know how the following story ended.

On a blustery grey summer afternoon in 1950, I heard the faint noise of a large, very low-flying aircraft, getting louder as it approached. There was a sudden blast of sound as a Valetta hove into view above a line of trees, so low that the

G-APAZ was one of two British civil Varsities, starting life as WF416   *B Robertson*

details could be clearly picked out such as windows, control surfaces and oil coolers. The big machine was bouncing around in the gusting conditions. But, much more significant, it was flying on one engine, which sounded as though it was being pressed hard to keep the Valetta aloft. In an instant it was all over with the machine receding into the distance, and all was quiet once more. But did the Valetta make it safely to the nearest airfield? A question I still ponder. The location was Danehill, Sussex. Perhaps it was just low-flying single-engine practice (lightly loaded), but this seems highly unlikely in view of the risks involved. If this bird was in trouble, I hope it landed safely.

A problem affecting Valettas was discovered when the RAF's VL282 crashed on 20 January 1954, taking off from RAF Lyneham bound for Istres in the South of France. The aircraft belonged to 30 Sqn at RAF Dishforth, but was being used for checking out signallers. At take-off, the aircraft climbed and stalled, and completed a number of "round outs", during the final one of which it hit the ground. The wings and engines were torn off and came to rest about 30 yards (27 m) away from the fuselage; fortunately there was no fire, although petrol was everywhere. The problem was quickly identified as the elevators being jammed in the up position; the needle roller bearings supporting the elevator motion were prepacked for life with grease on assembly, but the grease dried out over time and so the bearing seized. Other Valettas were found to have the problem, as did a number of BEA Vikings. From then on, maintenance involved regularly greasing the bearings. Sadly, the accident resulted in loss of life and injury, although some of the occupants escaped injury.

No less than 210 Valetta C Mk 1s were ordered, delivered from March 1948 to January 1952, and the type served in various parts of the world some of which included the Suez Canal Zone, Malaya and Kuwait. As a freighter, the Valetta C Mk 1 could take a 8,835 lb (4,008 kg) load comprising freight and lashings, examples of alternative loads being: two jeeps and drivers, one jeep and a carriage-mounted 25-pdr gun, one jeep and two trailers, etc. The troop transport version of the C Mk 1 could take 34 fully-armed troops, and included sound-proofing, WC and catering as well as an oxygen supply for flying at high altitudes. The paratrooper Valetta carried 20 paratroops and six 350 lb (159 kg) containers, while the ambulance version accommodated 20 stretchers, two sitting cases and two medical orderlies.

The supply dropping Valetta could take 12 x 350 lb (159 kg) containers manoeuvred on a double track roller conveyer, and three dispatchers. Finally, this versatile, reliable and roomy aircraft could also tow two sizeable gliders, but although a Valetta is shown being used as a glider tug on page 16, I never saw a Valetta working in this role in service. At high

Although quite clean, the Varsity's ventral pannier makes a rotund aircraft look even chubbier *M J Hooks*

payloads, the Valetta's range was correspondingly reduced, and as a freighter, range was down to only 357 miles (574 km). Three other versions of the Valetta included the C Mk 2, T Mk 3 and T Mk 4. The C Mk 2 was a VIP version seating up to 15 passengers and included a WC, pantry and baggage space. The Valetta T Mk 3 first flew on 31 August 1950 and was a navigational flying classroom for 10 students, and could be distinguished by its six roof-mounted astrodomes. Finally, a number T Mk 3s were converted to T Mk 4s for airborne interception radar training.

The other Viking development was the Varsity, visually having far less in common with the Viking than had the Valetta. The Varsity was much more streamlined than both Viking and Valetta, and had a nosewheel undercarriage, as well as beautifully cowled engines. It is tempting to conjecture that, with a pressurised cabin – which it did not have – the

One of the three Varsity prototypes in serene flight *B Robertson*

Viking might have been more like a Varsity if there had been less pressure to provide a stop-gap airliner for immediate post-war use. The Varsity first flew on 17 July 1949 as VX828, designed to replace the Wellington T10, a carryover from WW2 used as a trainer post-war, and the Valetta T Mks 3 and 4. The Varsity weighed 1,000 lb (454 kg) more than the Valetta; its span went up by 6 ft 5 ins (1.96 m) and its Hercules 264s produced 1,950 hp, reducing the Varsity's power loading below the Valetta's

Although they peaked at the same 2,800 rpm as the

Another shot of prototype Varsity VX828 showing undercarriage detail and tail bumper *Aeroplane*

Valetta's Herc 230s, the Varsity's engines had two-sped superchargers for altitude performance, and, to complement their supremely elegant clover-leaf cowlings, the Varsity's engines were given cylinder head seals to suit this type of enclosure. Anyone who has heard a Varsity in action might well feel that never has an aircraft with so many cylinders sounded as though it had so few! The Varsity's exhaust system conspired to make the Varsity sound rough and primitive, although it took the edge off the noise. Clover leaf cowlings gave good accessibility, and, on production aircraft, mainwheel undercarriage doors closed after lowering to cover the void and reduce drag when the landing gear was down.

A distinguishing feature of the Varsity, which made this rotund aircraft look even chubbier, was its ventral pannier for bomb-aimer training, also housing 24 small practice bombs (25 lb (11.3 kg) each). Small mudguards were fitted to the twin-nose wheels to stop the bombsight window being obscured by dirt thrown off by the tyres. The Varsity entered service with the RAF in 1951. The type was a general purpose RAF aircrew trainer, training pilots who would fly such aircraft as Hastings, Shackleton and others, and, in addition to bomb aimers, the Varsity also trained navigators, serving the RAF into the 'seventies. A total of 163 Varsities were built, mostly at Hurn while others, including the three prototypes, were built at Weybridge.

The prototype Varsity VX828 is shown in some of these shots, and, having first flown on 17 July 1949, this machine lasted until around 1962 when it was dismantled at Farnborough. Three Varsity prototypes were built, and the second one, VX835, first flew on 21 May 1950. After a spell with Vickers as a trials aircraft, VX835 was converted in 1953 to a test-bed for the Napier Eland turboprop.

Bizarrely, in its initial test-bed form VX835 retained its Hercules piston engine in the port nacelle, with an Eland in the starboard one. In due course two Elands were fitted. This Varsity was one of three aircraft converted to a test-bed for the Napier Eland NE1.1, the other two being a Convair 340 and Ambassador. Weighing 1,661 lb (753 kg), the Eland weighed 72 per cent of the Varsity's 2,305 lb (1,046 kg) Herc 764, yet the turboprop Eland was a full 57 per cent more powerful than the Hercules, with its 3,060 ehp compared to the Herc's 1,950 hp. With figures like these, coupled with the turboprops' simplicity and its quiet, smooth running, it was no wonder that Napier hoped to sell Eland conversions for piston-engined airliners. But the demand for turboprop conversions was less than hoped for, and only a relatively small number of Convairs received Elands, some as conversions and others as new airframes. The Eland was discontinued in 1962, and is barely remembered today. The Eland-Varsity aircraft was eventually sold to the College of Aeronautics at Cranfield for ground training, being gradually cannibalised for spares.

The above photo of the first prototype Varsity shows a number of interesting details. Apart from its ventral pannier the Varsity, although portly, has a clean form. The oil coolers can be seen slung under each engine, while the air intake to each engine, although not obvious from this photo, is blended in with the top of the cowling, as shown in the two photos on page 26. The discreet-looking cooling air and exhaust exits are in line with the rear of the engine cowling, and the cowling is almost turboprop-like in its aerodynamic cleanliness. The relationship with the Viking is evident from the wing and tail surface shape. Altogether, despite its Wellington ancestry, the Varsity is very much a post-war aircraft. The lower pictures

Family likeness - from this angle, the Valetta looks very like a Varsity *Aeroplane*

on pages 17 and 26 show the roof glazing given to both the Valetta and Varsity – absent from the Viking - giving them a military flavour.

Civil-registered Varsities were rare, and G-APAZ, one of the two British civil machines, is shown on page 25; the other machine was G-ARFP. G-APAZ first flew on 22 May 1952 as WF415. After its time with the RAF this Varsity was transferred to the Ministry of Supply and registered G-APAZ on 15 April 1957. It was operated from Staverton Aerodrome, near Gloucester, by Smiths Aviation Division. The Varsity was re-registered in November 1960 to the Ministry of Aviation and ended its days on 27 March 1963 when it crashed into a house in Gloucester during a pilot check flight from Staverton, following engine problems. Two people died in the accident. This was one of several Varsity losses, but a particularly unusual incident occurred to Varsity WF246 on 26 April 1955 when an airframe mechanic, not qualified to pilot an aircraft, managed to make an unauthorised flight to France.

To digress, I spent many happy hours at Staverton Aerodrome aircraft spotting during the mid to late 'fifties. I never saw the Varsity there. The most common machines then were various types of Auster, and Tiger Moth G-ANER was also based there, as was a green Miles Monarch or Whitney Straight – I forget which. Most interesting was an Anson with a radar nose, presumably used for research, and seeing it take-off was a rare treat as it was one of the largest aircraft there. The Anson's Cheetah engines running at high power just after take-off sounded magnificent, while, in comparison, the harsh crackle from the Cirrus Minor engines fitted to some of the Austers sounded unpleasant – a lot of low-quality noise for such a small engine! Just occasionally, we also saw a Cambrian Airways DC-3.

Staverton was also the venue for what we used to call the Staverton Sprint, an organised motor sprint event using the perimeter track. Some magnificent cars were entered, some of them supercharged and most of them fast, ranging from pre-war to current. Perhaps the two which come to most to mind from all those years ago was a pre-war Bugatti Type 35C racing car, as well as a "special" powered by a de Havilland Gypsy Major engine, presumably ex-Tiger Moth, deafeningly noisy, but not very fast. There was an added bonus from the magnificent sight of Gloucester Cathedral in the distance rising above its surroundings - an inspiring sight. I made many visits to this ancient Cathedral at that time.

Now, back to Varsities! Varsity WL679 was a common sight flying around the Farnborough area for many years and I remember it well, having first seen it when it went to Farnborough in 1954. This Varsity was one of the last batch of 50 ordered by the Air Ministry for delivery during 1952/3, and was built at Hurn. This aircraft was delivered to 8 MU on 2 October 1953, but it was not used by the RAF, and on 14 January 1954 it joined the Empire Test Pilot's School, Farnborough, where it worked for 14 years with the School. WL679 then went to Royal Aircraft Establishment (RAE) Pershore on 29 August 1968 for use in radar trials. It then went to Little Broughton where it was resparred, and then back to Pershore in April 1970.

By July 1973, the Varsity's work for Pershore had come to an end, and it was scheduled to for use in fire-fighting practice, fortunately it went, instead, to RAE Farnborough, delivered on 13 July 1973. Then it moved to West Malling until late March 1977, then back to Farnborough. Trials equipment was installed, for research involving infra-red, thermal imaging and thermal detection systems. The Varsity, despite its old design, proved to be an ideal trials platform. One morning I was walking through Farnham in Surrey, and I saw WL679 flying overhead, and with half-closed eyes I could almost imagine that it was a WW2 Wellington from the shapes of the wings and tail plane. But the Varsity's "modern" Hercs sounded quite different, gruff and rough-sounding compared to the Wellington's smoother noise. The last I saw of the *Flying Pig* as this Varsity was called, was in 1991 or so, flying low over Alton, Hampshire, resplendent in its immaculate finish. Not long afterwards it was withdrawn from service after 38 years in RAF roundels and is now preserved at Cosford Aerospace Museum.

Although the Varsity was designed as a trainer, Vickers considered producing a short/medium haul airliner version, but with the much superior Viscount then being developed, a superb airliner as it turned out, the Varsity airliner was not proceeded with. The nearest American aircraft with which a Varsity airliner would have competed was the Convair 240, but the Convair twin was a larger and more powerful aircraft and the Varsity was actually much nearer to the Viking than the Convair. If the Viking had been in the mould of the Varsity instead of the less sophisticated machine that it was, with a pressurised cabin and reversible pitch propellers which the Convair had, it would have been interesting to see how this might have affected sales

Used Vikings entered service with independent airlines such as Autair, Eagle, Hunting Clan and Tradair, among others. The majority of Vikings changed hands more than once and went to operators in Great Britain and overseas; they served in diminishing numbers until by 1970 they had practically all been withdrawn. During my aircraft spotting visits to Blackbushe, there was a motley collection of ageing machines in service, Vikings, Hermes, Yorks, DC-3s, and Argonauts going about their daily duties and the locality reverberated to the sound of Hercules, Merlins and Twin Wasps. Other machines included the odd Viscount, an Airspeed Consul, Beechcraft 18 and, of all things, a Lincoln, among others. When I took the 'O' Level French oral exam during the Summer of 1957, I mentioned an airport I had visited (in my best French) and the examiner seized on this and asked if I had seen any "Veekeengs". This, he thought, was how Viking should be pronounced in French. Not being very sure myself, I went along with it and, in order to stay on familiar territory, I assured him that I had seen some "Veekeengs"!

Several examples of the Viking/Valetta/Varsity have been preserved. One, in particular, was rescued from a rather undignified existence for an airliner! Viking 498 Mk 1A G-AGRU first flew on 19 July 1946 and was delivered to BEA as *Vagrant* (surely a better name than this could have been chosen!). G-AGRU was converted to a Mk 1 after her time with BEA – with stressed skin metal wings and, I suspect, a rear exhaust ring which it now has – and thereafter served with a number of operators ending up in Sosterberg, Holland in 1964, when she was withdrawn from use and used as a coffee shop! Tables and chairs were placed in the passenger cabin for the customers and the cockpit had been stripped of its equipment which was replaced by a cooking stove, but fortunately G-AGRU was acquired for restoration in 1979 and went on display at Cosford Aerospace Museum in its former BEA colours. *Vagrant* has now been moved "home" to Brooklands Museum, Weybridge.

The Viking never had any pretensions to being a modern airliner, with its lack of pressurisation, tailwheel undercarriage and relatively small capacity. However it was available immediately after WW2 when it was needed, its gestation period being shortened by basing it on the proven wartime Wellington bomber, so the Viking was in essence thoroughly "sorted" from the start. It was never intended to compete with up to the minute designs such as the Convair 240 and Airspeed Ambassador. But the Viking proved to be a fine airliner and was good enough to remain in demand by operators for over 20 years after going out of production.

I look back on my Viking flights with pleasure, having a love-hate with the aircraft because on the one hand it was British and until 1952 the only British post-war medium-size airliner in service, and it carried the British torch at a time when American airliners dominated world markets. But the Viking's fuselage detracted from its looks from any angle, and it looked grotesque from some. Its inferiority in performance and concept to the glamorous American Convair was most frustrating. But we British redressed the balance in 1953 when the Viking's superb successor, the turboprop Viscount, went into service and took the world's commercial operators by storm.

✱✱✱✱✱✱✱✱✱✱✱✱

Technical Data

*VICKERS VIKING 610 MK 1B**

Manufacturer:	Vickers Armstrongs Ltd, Weybridge, Surrey, UK.
Type:	Twin-engined short/medium-haul airliner.
Wings:	Cantilever mid-wing monoplane. Inner sections have geodetic frames skinned with unstressed Alclad. Outer sections are stressed-skin all-metal structures.
Tail unit:	Cantilever monoplane type with single fin. All-metal structure, except fabric-covered elevators and rudder.
Fuselage:	All-metal structure.
Accommodation:	Flight crew comprises pilot, co-pilot/radio operator and navigator. Side-by-side dual control. One cabin attendant. Cabin for 24/27 passengers in pairs to starboard and singly to port, separated by offset aisle. Galley and WC at rear. Unpressurised accommodation. Under-floor freight hold with external loading doors.
Engines:	Two Bristol Hercules 634 fourteen cylinder aircooled radial engines. De Havilland or Rotol constant-speed, four-blade, feathering propellers; no reversible pitch. Each engine gives 1,690 hp for take-off @ 2,800 rpm, and normal climb power of 1,510 hp @ 2,400 RPM @ 3,750 ft (1,143 m).
Landing Gear:	Retractable tailwheel landing gear with single main wheel on each side. Hydraulic retraction, mainwheels into engine nacelles; retractable tailwheel.
Dimensions:	Span 89 ft 3 in (27.2 m), length 65 ft 2 in (19.86 m), tail-down height 19 ft 6 in (5.94 m). Wing area 882 ft^2 (81.94 m^2). Propeller diameter 13 ft 3 in (4.04 m). Main-wheel track 22 ft 10 in (6.96 m), wheel-base 33 ft 5 in (10.19 m).
Weights & Loadings:	Empty 22,910 lb (10,392 kg) for 24-passenger layout, and 23,000 lb (10,433 kg) for 27-passengers. Maximum take-off 34,000 lb (15,422 kg). Maximum landing 32,500 lb (14,742 kg).
Performance:	Cruising speed 210 mph (338 km/h) using 775 hp per engine. Range 1,700 miles (2,735 km) @ 210 mph (338 km/h), with 750 Imperial gallons (3,410 litres) of fuel. Rate of climb 1,500 ft/min (457 m/min) @ 3,000 ft (914 m) @ 34,000 lb (15,422 kg).

* Supplied to British European Airways

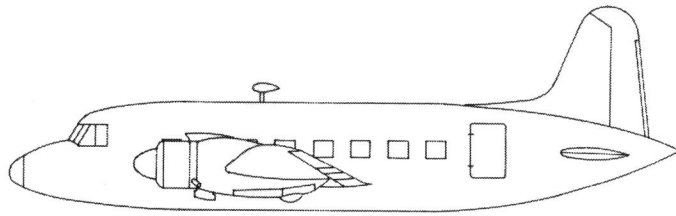

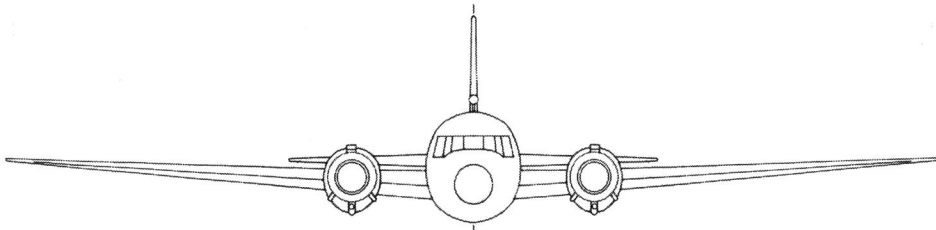

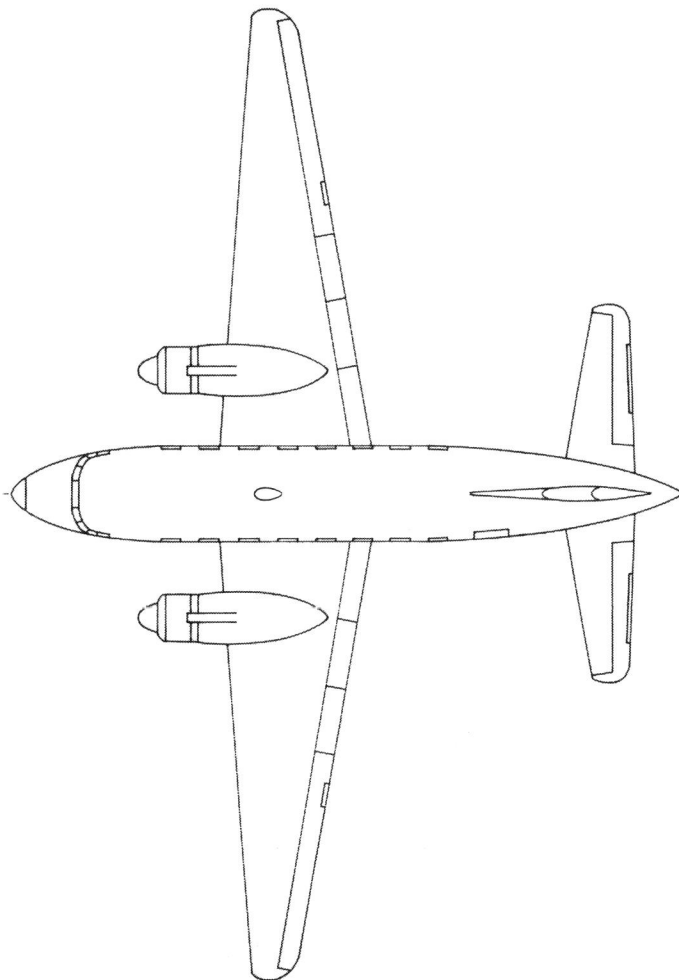

0   20 ft

0   4 m

VICKERS VIKING Mk 1B

© N J B Corrie 2003

Technical Data

BRISTOL HERCULES 634 ENGINE

Manufacturer: Bristol Aeroplane Company Ltd (Engine Division), Filton, Bristol, UK.

Type: 14-cylinder aircooled, two-row, radial piston engine.

Cylinders: Bore 5.75 in (146 mm), stroke 6.50 in (165 mm), total swept volume 2,363 in^3 (38.7 litres).

Connecting Rods: Each cylinder row has master rod; six auxillary rods are connected to each master rod.

Crankshaft: Two-throw three-piece crankshaft is supported by roller main bearings.

Crankcase: Comprises three sections.

Valvegear: Single crank-driven sleeve valve per cylinder.

Induction: Single-speed single-stage supercharger is fitted at rear of engine. Centrifugal impeller is driven by step-up epicyclic gearing from crankshaft.

Lubrication: Dry-sump system with forced feed throughout engine by oil pump.

Ignition: Spark ignition system fitted, comprising two independent magneto-energised systems. Two spark plugs per cylinder.

Propeller Drive: Reduction gear of 0.444:1 ratio.

Dimensions: Diameter 52 in (1.32 m).

Dry Weight: 1,945 lb (882 kg).

Performance: Take-off power: 1,690 hp @ 2,800 RPM. Normal climb power: 1,510 hp @ 2,400 RPM @ 3,750 ft (1,143 m). Maximum economical cruise power: 1,315 hp @ 2,400 rpm @ 8,250 ft (2,515 m).